The publishers would like to thank the following oa
providing colour illustrations:– John Howard; E. D. Lacey,
Richard H. Parker; Mike Roberts; Peter Roberts Editorial &
Photographic; Sport & General Press Agency; Syndication
International Limited. The illustration on page 21 was
supplied by Roy Pembrooke from the London Weekend
Television series *The Adventures of Black Beauty.*

Published 1975 by
The Hamlyn Publishing Group Limited
London · New York · Sydney · Toronto
Astronaut House, Feltham, Middlesex, England
© Copyright The Hamlyn Publishing Group Limited 1975
ISBN 0 600 33101 6
Printed in England by Tinling (1973) Ltd,
Prescot, Merseyside.

SUCCESSFUL Riding and Jumping

By Robert Owen

Illustrated by Gwen Green

Hamlyn

London · Sydney · New York · Toronto

CONTENTS

INTRODUCTION

More and more young people throughout the world are developing an increasing interest in all aspects of riding. This book will appeal to all who love horses and ponies and especially to those who appreciate the need for schooling and, who want to learn more about the technique of riding.

SUCCESSFUL RIDING AND JUMPING sets out to teach you techniques necessary to develop the skills required to ride well. The importance of schooling is stressed (for both pony *and* rider!) and some useful exercises are given for you to practise. Special attention, however, is paid to the finer points of jumping, since jumping has now become such a popular international pastime. You will find basic training methods described, the use and importance of cavalletti and the value of properly-constructed schooling fences. You will learn about some of the problems riders face in competitive jumping and the various types of obstacles used in both show jumping and cross-country events.

To be a successful rider does not mean that you must know all there is to know about equitation. That will never happen! The subject is far too broad and complex. A measure of success, however, will be achieved by those who apply three basic principles to their everyday riding: sympathy, patience and, above all, understanding. They are essential if you are to enjoy the fun and pleasure of riding to the full.

BITS AND BRIDLES

The bit is used to control the energy of a pony which is built up in the quarters by the correct use of the rider's legs, body and seat.

The reins are used to make contact with the pony's mouth and these serve as a link between the bit and the rider's hands. When you increase contact with your hands (usually by opening or closing them) the pony will relax his jaw. He is then brought up to the bit by applying the aids (see page 12). Your hands will then be able to regulate the energy and the pony will move at the pace you choose.

Your hands are also used to direct the pony, but they should never be used without the other natural aids. For successful riding and jumping it is essential that your hands are gentle.

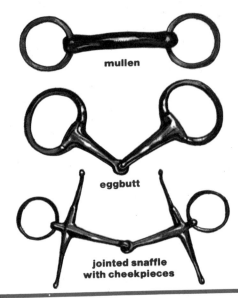

mullen

eggbutt

jointed snaffle
with cheekpieces

The Snaffle is a form of bit used in all riding disciplines. It is an excellent bit for both horses and ponies since, when properly fitted, it is both kind and gentle to their mouths. There are several types, and the two most commonly used are the "jointed" snaffle, and the "half-moon" or "mullen".

The jointed snaffle is made from metal and acts on the corners of the mouth. The mullen, with its straight bar, can be made from vulcanite, rubber or metal. Some snaffle bits, like the "eggbutt" illustrated, do not have loose rings and are, therefore, less likely to pinch any part of the lips or corners of the mouth.

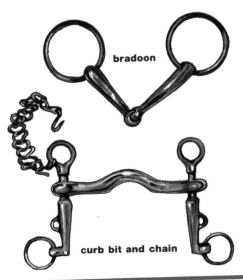

bradoon

curb bit and chain

The Double Bridle is a more advanced form of bitting and should not be introduced unless expert advice and guidance has been given. The double bridle is a combination of a "bradoon" bit, "curb" bit and curb chain. The action of the curb chain, shown on page 9, makes the pony bend his head inwards from the poll: the bradoon raises the head to the right position. Great care must be taken when using the curb rein because this bitting arrangement can be severe on the pony's mouth if not completely understood.

Pelham

Kimblewick

The Pelham very popular with younger riders, combines the actions of a snaffle and a double bridle. This bridle has two reins which make one bit do the work of two, and it is, therefore, a difficult arrangement to handle well. In a single mouthpiece it comprises a snaffle bit with a curb chain. As such, it is not nearly so efficient as the bitting arrangement of the double bridle which it attempts to copy. The Kimblewick, one of the several groups found in the Pelham family uses a single rein.

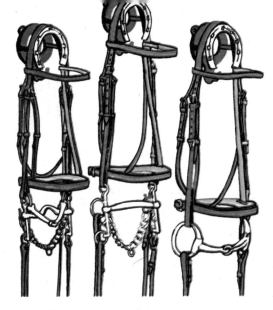

Bridle Care. To "put up" a bridle, run the reins through the throat lash, keeping the noseband outside the cheek pieces. Do not buckle the noseband, simply slide the strap through the keeper and runner. Make sure the reins are not twisted and hang it carefully so that it keeps its correct shape. Always clean your bridle before putting it up.

Nosebands

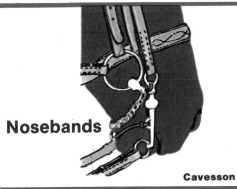

Cavesson

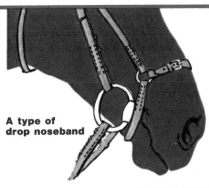

A type of drop noseband

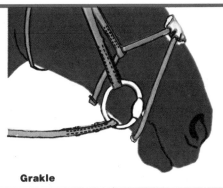

Grakle

The normal position of a Pelham.

The action of the curb-chain when the curb rein is used.

1. Before the headcollar is removed, put the reins over the pony's neck.

3. See that the tongue is under the bit and the bridle, correctly adjusted.

2. Hold headpiece and gently guide bit into the mouth with the left hand.

4. Buckle all the straps and check the space between head and throatlash.

SADDLERY

In the show ring a well-turned out pony is essential: in the jumping ring this is equally important as it also shows that the saddlery or "tack" is safe and will not cause an accident. Badly fitting tack is unsafe for the rider and unkind to the pony, so be sure that it fits properly and that you are suitably dressed on all occasions.

Remember to clean and inspect your tack regularly—it is one of the most important parts of equitation. Cleaning will keep the leather supple and prevent it from becoming cracked. By inspecting it frequently you will ensure that the leather is safe and the stitching, usually the part to disintegrate, secure.

When fitting a new or a secondhand saddle look closely to make sure that no part of it is resting on the pony's loins or spine—the weight must be taken on the muscles which cover the upper part of the ribs. You must also check that there is no pinching when the pommel is placed just behind the rise of the withers.

Next, look at the condition of the stuffing of the saddle. This can be the cause of much discomfort and should be inspected by a saddler at least once a year.

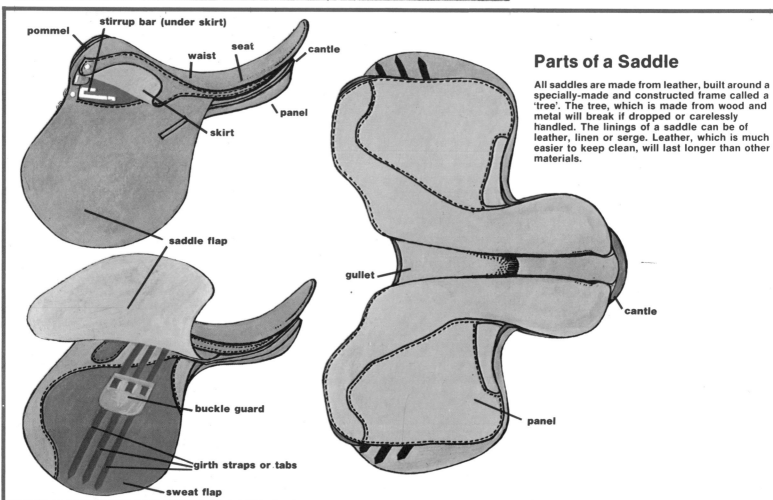

Parts of a Saddle

All saddles are made from leather, built around a specially-made and constructed frame called a 'tree'. The tree, which is made from wood and metal will break if dropped or carelessly handled. The linings of a saddle can be of leather, linen or serge. Leather, which is much easier to keep clean, will last longer than other materials.

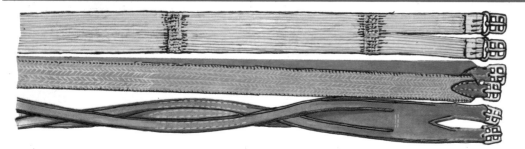

Girths

Left (top): A nylon cord girth, both inexpensive and most satisfactory. *(middle):* A webbing girth. These are always used in pairs. *(bottom):* a leather girth, which is considered best of all materials. It is strong and less likely to stretch.

Saddling-Up

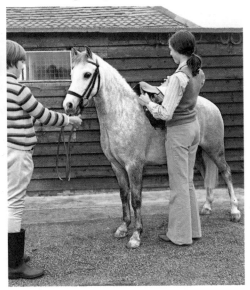

1. Always saddle-up on the nearside. Place the saddle lightly on the pony's back, and forward on the withers. Gently slide the saddle down to the correct position.

2. Check that the saddle flaps are down on both sides, and that all is smooth and flat under the flaps. If you use a saddle cloth or numnah this, too, must be checked.

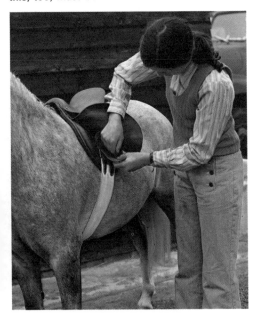

3. See that the girth buckles are level. Tighten these sufficiently to hold the saddle quite firmly. They must be tightened again once you have mounted and before moving off.

Two types of Saddle

A show saddle *(left)* and *(below)*, a general purpose saddle.

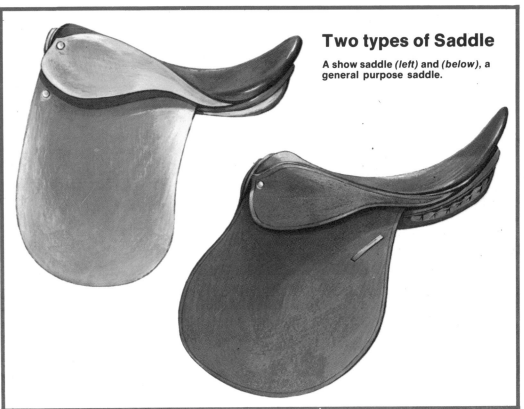

Protective and other Clothing

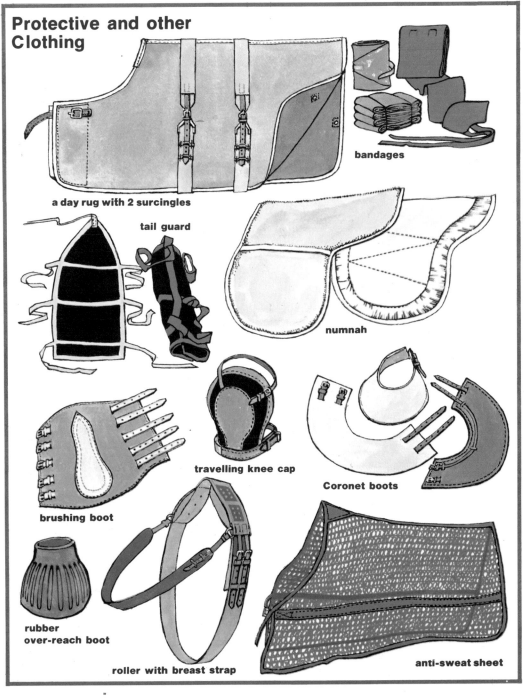

a day rug with 2 surcingles

bandages

tail guard

numnah

brushing boot

travelling knee cap

Coronet boots

rubber over-reach boot

roller with breast strap

anti-sweat sheet

AIDS

Aids are the signals or the language used to tell the pony what he should do. These fall into two groups: the natural aids are those signals passed by the rider to the pony by the correct use of the legs, body and seat to support the action given by the hands: the artificial aids include the stick, spurs and more complex pieces of saddlery such as martingales.

We explain here the aids in relation to "impulsion", "collection" and "extension"—three words used frequently at all levels of equitation and which riders must understand before moving to the more advanced stages of riding and jumping.

When aids are given, it is important that the pony understands the signal and obeys at once. With a young pony or one not used to his new owner this may not be easy at first and in the early stages of training the aids may need to be over-emphasised. In time, with care and patience you will find that he will respond immediately. All riders should

Above (left): **A rider correctly seated on a well-balanced horse at the halt position, ready to apply the natural aids to move forward.** *(right):* **the same horse and rider equipped with the artificial aids; whip, spurs, and martingale.**

know how the aids are given, what they are given for, what response should be received from the pony and how the rider can recognise those responses.

legs

hands

Natural Aids

LEGS, when correctly applied, create "impulsion", another word for the energy you build up behind the saddle in the pony's quarters. They also guide and give control to the hindquarters.
HANDS control impulsion. They will also help to guide and allow changes of pace if you apply them properly with the right supporting aids. When used with your legs and body, your hands control "collection", which tells you that energy has been built up. A forward movement by releasing some of the tension in the reins, will produce a collected pace and a slow, short stride. The opposite to collection is "extension". The head and neck are allowed more freedom, which will introduce an extended stride and a quicker pace.

The BODY, maintaining a straightened or braced spine, plays an important part in successful riding and jumping. Your body weight can affect the balance of your pony and a correct seat will tell

Artificial Aids

The WHIP or stick must not exceed 76 cm (30 ins.) when used in the show jumping ring. The stick can be used to reinforce the leg aids, but must never be used in front of the saddle.

SPURS are for the experienced rider, although they are recognised as one of the artificial aids. The length of the spur can vary, but younger riders should keep to the short necks. If these have curved necks they must point downwards; they must not be worn upside down.

MARTINGALES. The martingale is used to prevent the horse's head being carried too high. It is not for holding the head down. Properly fitted and used, martingales give a rider better control.

The running martingale, which has two rings to allow it to move freely along the reins, is preferred to the standing martingale. It is not as severe, but it should be introduced only after expert advice has been given.

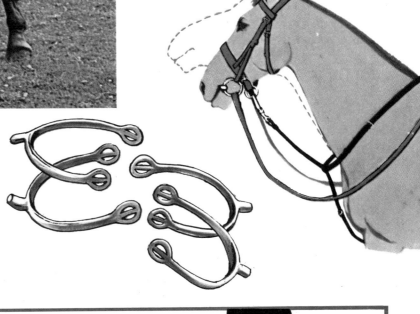

Above: Some whips and sticks. *(right):* stainless steel or nickel spurs made in the Prince of Wales pattern.

body

you whether or not the overall balance is being maintained. Through your seat you will also be able to feel the response you are getting to the aids you are giving.

voice

The VOICE should be used as calmly and as quietly as possible and should be used to encourage. Use the voice sharply, but sparingly, should a reprimand be necessary.

THE NATURAL PACES

A pony can adopt four natural paces or gaits: the walk, trot, canter and gallop. At a walk the pace is made up of four steps or beats; at the trot, two steps; at the canter, three steps and at the gallop, four steps. There are other paces used for jumping, where an adjustment to the stride is necessary, which include the "extended" and "collected" paces.

When you have mastered the correct way to apply the natural aids you should be able to move smoothly from one pace into another.

Walk

Before you mount, your pony must have been taught to stand quite still. Do not attempt to mount until he is quiet and obedient. After mounting, settle into the saddle and check the girth. Sit well down in the centre of the saddle, keeping your back straight but relaxed and look ahead. The knees and thighs should be kept close to the saddle with the lower part of the legs free. In the stirrup, the ball of the foot should rest against the bar with the heels positioned lower than the toes. With the reins, apply just a light contact with the pony's mouth.

You are now ready to give the aids to "walk on". Apply pressure by squeezing the lower part of your legs against the pony's sides to build up energy. Maintaining contact with you hands adjust your body weight and slightly

Trot

When moving from a walk to a trot, remain seated correctly and increase pressure with the lower part of the legs. Slightly shorten the reins to bring your pony well up to the bit and, as soon as he responds, squeeze your legs just enough to keep the pace. Now ease the reins, but maintain a light contact with the pony's mouth.

There are two ways of riding at a trot—"sitting" and "rising". The sitting trot is used when making the transition from one pace to another as it enables you to keep closer contact with your pony for better control.

The rising trot, where the rider rises up and down in the saddle, is the most comfortable "seat" for both pony and rider. Keeping the same body position as for the sitting trot—a straight back, don't lean forward—grip well with your

Canter

To move freely from a trot to a canter make sure your pony responds to the movements of both the walk and the trot. As in all paces, the pony should be well collected, and the rider must sense he will be responsive to pressures applied either through the legs or the reins. Sit upright and deeply into the saddle. Apply increased pressure with both legs just behind the girth. That, in simple terms, should produce a canter. In reality there is very much more to it than that!

The canter is a three beat pace and it is, therefore, possible for a pony to move into this stride from the near-fore or off-foreleg. A pony is said to be cantering "true" or "united" when the leading foreleg and leading hindleg are on the same side. If they appear on the opposite side, he is cantering "disunited". The body weight and balance of the rider can quickly upset a canter. If you lean too far forward, you will have little control, particularly if your mount

"open" your hands; the pony will be brought up to the bit and will move off. Remember, the hands control impulsion and the action of your hands are all important for an obedient and regulated movement.

To bring your pony to a halt, sit well into the saddle and straighten or brace the spine. Next, close the lower part of the legs and keep an equal pressure against the pony's sides. "Close" the hands sufficiently to bring him up to the bit. The pressure from your legs and the resistance the pony will feel through the bit will bring him quietly to a halt, standing square on all four legs.

Some ponies get into the habit of moving off as soon as their rider has mounted. They never wait for the correct aids and this habit must not be allowed to go unchecked. A pony must always obey the aids; never change your mind to suit his!

knees and thighs to help you rise up and down. Don't rely on the stirrups alone! Your legs should be quite still against the pony's sides and the hands level. To slow up, use the same aids as for the walk, and rein-in a little tighter if necessary. To bring your pony to a halt, close your legs and straighten the spine. You will find that some ponies walk one or two paces before finally stopping.

If you are trotting correctly, you are said to be "riding on the two diagonals" in a pace of two steps. The right diagonal refers to the action of the pony's off-fore and near-hind legs: the near-fore and off-hind refers to the left diagonal. You should be riding on the right diagonal when you come back into the saddle that is as the pony's off-fore and near-hind legs come to the ground. Always change the diagonal when you change reins and practise the changes when schooling and out hacking.

starts to move faster.

When cantering in a straight line it does not matter which leg leads. If you want to canter off with the off-fore leading (that is the right leg), use the right rein to incline the pony's head very slightly to the right. Your left leg is then applied behind the girth to prevent the pony's hindquarters from moving out. The right leg remains level with the girth and gives increased pressure to maintain the pace. To lead off with the foreleg, simply reverse the aids so that the pony's head inclines to the left, your left leg applies pressure on the girth and your right leg remains slightly behind it. When cantering in a circle (see page 20) the pressure of your inside leg, is used to keep up the impulsion and pace, while the outside leg controls the bend by preventing too much of a swing from the pony's quarters.

The canter, for both rider and pony, is a most difficult pace to perform really well but it should be practised, since it is used a great deal in riding.

EXERCISING

Each time you take your pony out, on the roads, along bridle paths, or across common land, he is being exercised. A pony will give himself some exercise, of course, when he is out at grass, particularly if he is with other animals. The time you give to exercising depends very much on what you set out to achieve with your pony and you should try to develop a programme that will benefit you both.

When exercising "feel" your balance is right. Learn to change legs and practise changes of rein. Bring your pony back to a halt and then move on using the correct aids and on the leg you choose. Make sure your pony is obedient to your aids and always do what you want to do—never the other way round! Occasionally practise the rein-back.

Riding on the road is a useful and beneficial exercise if not overdone. You should ride according to the Highway Code, and consider other road users at all times.

Above: **Some of the exercising movements and figures that can be made in a ménage or schooling arena. The illustration shows circles of 10m. (11 yds) diameter; some tighter circles and how to position for figures of eight, using the main part of the arena. Lateral and diagonals from the outside tracks are also shown.**

Schooling and exercising must always cover some specific training movement for which it is advisable to seek expert advice. By all means practise what you are taught, but never attempt any advanced training without guidance.

To improve the balance and obedience of a pony a ménage or schooling ring in the corner of a field or paddock is extremely valuable. This can be formed by making use of a hedge or fence on two sides and railing or roping off two inside markers. Straw bales can be a useful guide to contain the school. Ideally, the fenced-in area should measure 40 metres by 20 metres (44 yards by 22 yards) and the ground should be as flat as possible. The proper use of the area will go a long way to improve the suppleness and balance of your pony and, at the same time, will do much to teach him to observe and obey the aids given.

Schooling should begin at a walk, crossing and re-crossing the diagonals and making all the necessary changes of rein in the proper way! Use your legs at the corners do not expect your pony to turn without first giving him the aids. Keep your inside leg pushing him forward and the outside leg preventing a swing from his quarters. Don't forget that schooling is just as important for you as for your pony, so sit properly and don't allow lazy habits to develop!

Once you feel you have your pony's full attention, he has come up to the bit and he appears to have settled in the schooling area, you can begin specific exercises such as circles, figures of eight, serpentines and diagonals. Occasionally bring your pony away from the inside edge of the school—about 2 metres (6 feet) from the edge so that you can check that you are receiving obedience from the aids you are giving. Even in an enclosed schooling area your pony will find it difficult to act solely on the aids and resist using the arena markers as a guiding edge to cling to! During schooling maintain im-

pulsion. Where you can, keep the pony straight and see that he pays attention. Vary your paces and use this exercise and schooling time to develop suppleness.

The normal track in a ménage or school.

The track here has been brought away from the edge, making it more difficult for both pony and rider.

RIDING A CIRCLE

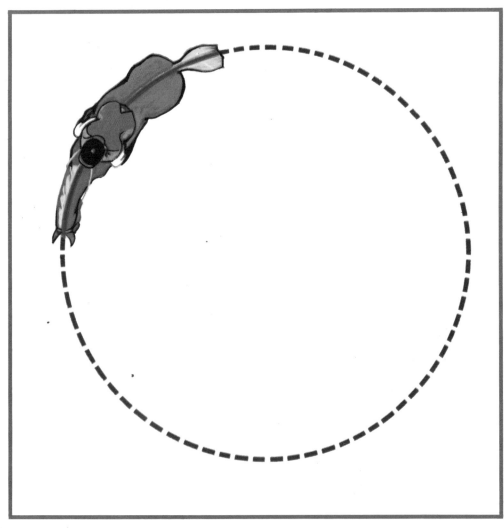

To ride a circle the pony's spine should be in line with the circumference of the circle being made. You may find it difficult to know whether or not your pony is carrying out a true circle, something fairly easy to judge in a ménage or school but extremely hard when, for example, you are in the show ring. The onlooker, however, sees it all very clearly! If the pony is moving as it should, his hind feet will follow in the footprints of the forefeet. Depending on the pace, they may sometimes reach over the prints, but they must never stray from one side to the other.

When trotting, it is preferable to use a small circle no less than 10 metres (11 yards) in diameter, and a circle not more than 20 metres (22 yards) in diameter when cantering; this induces a more active use of the hindlegs so that they will bend accurately into the line being taken.

After riding circles, serpentines or loops should be attempted. Providing the loops themselves are not too deep, this is a valuable suppling exercise, and one that can be practised at the walk, trot or canter.

Never hurry any part of your schooling. Take everything calmly, but do not repeat the same exercise too often. Variety is good for both rider and pony!

A serpentine or loop.

LUNGEING

The object of lungeing is to teach obedience; to help develop muscles on both sides; to encourage a free forward movement at different paces and to improve a pony's balance. Young riders should not lunge unless they really know what they are doing. It is best to take advice from those with experience which, of course, applies to all facets of riding.

Lungeing is carried out by the trainer, who stands in the centre of a circle with the rein in his leading hand. That is his left hand when the pony circles to the left and the right hand when circling to the right. The trainer has a lunge whip which is "shown" to the pony on commands such as "walk on" or "trot on". The pony will quickly learn to link the words with the sight of the whip, knowing that the whip will not be used.

The webbing lunge rein is attached to a specially made and carefully fitted noseband called a "cavesson". The trainer coaxes the pony to undertake a variety of exercises at different paces. Should the pony set off in a canter on the wrong leg, he should be brought back to the trot and started again. Lungeing should not be carried out for too long at a time—about twenty minutes is advisable—dividing the time equally between circling to the right and left.

At the close of each lungeing session you should reward your pony. Some grass or a few nuts will be sufficient. Some reward should also be given when he has carried out your instructions during a lesson – this is best given by thanking him with words, rather than titbits.

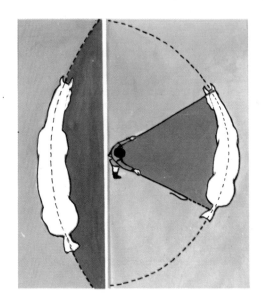

Far left: A correct Cavesson noseband has been fitted before beginning a lungeing lesson. *(left):* The correct position of the hands when lungeing to the left.

JUMPING

Most ponies, when jumping free, without tack and without a rider, show their skill in their determined approach to an obstacle. In fact, ponies go out of their way to jump; they would rather do that than have to go round something in their path! It is in carrying a rider and maintaining balance, that problems arise.

If you look at pictures of a horse jumping free you will find that he places himself at the right position for take-off, having approached the obstacle at the required speed. Well-trained horses will jump high fences at a trot, provided they are balanced and well-positioned.

As a horse approaches the jump he lowers his head to enable him to judge the height by focussing on a ground line. This is explained (right). Next, he stretches his neck to assist his balance. At the position of take-off he shortens his neck and gathers his hocks well under his body. Next he lifts his forelegs and his impulsion drives him up and over.

At the time of suspension over the jump he stretches his head and neck again. On landing, he brings his head up and shortens his neck. His forelegs, as they land, control his balance. The hind legs come down almost in the footprints of the forelegs and he collects, adjusts his balance and moves off.

On the following pages we describe the jumping process and the problems facing both horse and rider.

Balance, as you will now know, is the basic element required for all riding. A pony is balanced when his weight and the weight of his rider is evenly spread over each leg to enable him to use himself with the greatest of ease in all paces. Balance, therefore, is a question of distribution of weight. We can understand how simple it is for a horse or pony jumping free to produce his own well-balanced movements. The problem he faces is when a rider is added to his back!

Since balance is the most important part of riding, it is essential that you understand what this means. Good show jumping is a partnership. The pony can be brilliant, but only moderate results will come to a rider who does not understand the basic principles of jumping and does not want to learn.

When jumping, your body should remain as still as possible and the back, straight but supple. Your shoulders and back should be positioned slightly forward and the weight taken on the knees and thighs, not on the stirrups. You must be sure to jump with your

continued on page 22

This obstacle has no ground line. A pony would find it difficult to judge its height.

The same obstacle with a ground line. To jump this, a pony could focus on the ground line and judge the height of the fence.

Jumping Free

ground line focus point

1

2

1 taking-off

2 suspension

3 descent

4 point of touch down

JUMPING

leathers shortened. This helps you to balance yourself and gives you an opportunity for a better grip. You may find that two or three holes shorter than you have when hacking will give you about the right length. Keep your head looking in the direction you are taking—never, never look down as you jump, this will only upset the balance. Maintain your body balance by using the knees and thighs. The lower part of your legs must remain close to the sides of the pony.

Your arms should remain close to your body and must be relaxed sufficiently to enable them to follow the movement of the head and neck of the pony. When you give and ask for an extension, your arms, shoulders and body must follow the movement.

In the early stages, when jumping over low poles or across a line of cavalletti (see page 26) you should continually practise and use the correct jumping position. If you do, you will find that you will adopt this position quite naturally when you come to jump proper fences—there is quite enough to remember when jumping without having to work out your body position!

When the pony rises at the jump your body weight should be slightly forward; you should move further forward as the pony stretches his neck and your arms follow. But remember, always maintain contact with the mouth. The position of your body as you rise over a jump should allow your weight to be spread evenly—you must not allow all your weight to remain on the loins, as it would if you sat back in your seat.

On landing be careful not to bounce back in the saddle. As the pony touches down he will raise his head. You must avoid the tendency here to sit back before regaining the correct jumping position.

A pony will jump when he is asked to approach the obstacle at an even pace and when everything else is right! As discussed earlier, a pony jumping free will arrive at the right point for take-off and will have balanced himself before and after the jump. Most bad jumping occurs when the riders expect their ponies to correct any errors in the approach and then, somehow, to adjust their balance. Practise and careful schooling is part of the answer; experience gained is another.

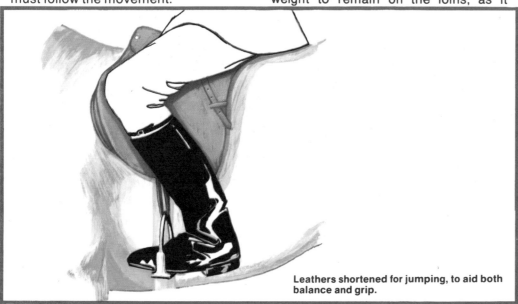

Leathers shortened for jumping, to aid both balance and grip.

1. As you arrive at the point of take-off you must have both balance and the correct impulsion. It is now too late to make any adjustment. Keep close contact with your seat, hands and legs.

2. As the horse rises you must keep the jumping position and follow closely the movements of the horse. Do not allow your own weight to fall back.

3. At the point of suspension, prepare yourself for landing and collection. Look ahead, never look down. Maintain contact with your hands and legs.

4. When landing, adjust your hands and arms to keep contact, and bring your body back gently to regain contact with your seat.

5. When your pony has landed, "collect" and revert to the normal position. Remember – your horse is the one that is jumping; you are being carried! Be considerate and sympathetic – not a burden.

3

4

5

SCHOOLING OVER POLES

When learning to jump and in the early stages of a new partnership, it is necessary to develop confidence between pony and rider. One of the best ways to start is to walk and trot across a number of coloured poles which have been laid on the ground. Depending on the stride of your pony these should be placed about 152 centimetres (5 feet) apart.

At the beginning of a schooling period you must walk, giving your hands to the pony as he lowers his head and stretches his neck at each pole. Then try trotting, making sure to maintain an even pace. Never overdo this or any other part of your exercising or schooling plans. When your pony does well, make a fuss of him and move onto another type of exercise.

Once you feel happy about the poles on the ground, raise them on bricks to a height of 8 centimetres (3 inches) and again go through the routine. The next stage, in all probability, will be the use of cavalletti with the lowest height of 25 centimetres (10 inches).

Opposite: When schooling over poles it is sometimes useful to have three or four ponies following each other. If you do this you must keep to a regular distance between each other and not allow any pony to move up to the one in front.

After one pony has lead for a while, change the order. Be sure that whichever pace you choose – walk, trot or canter – each one maintains that pace throughout each phase of the exercise.

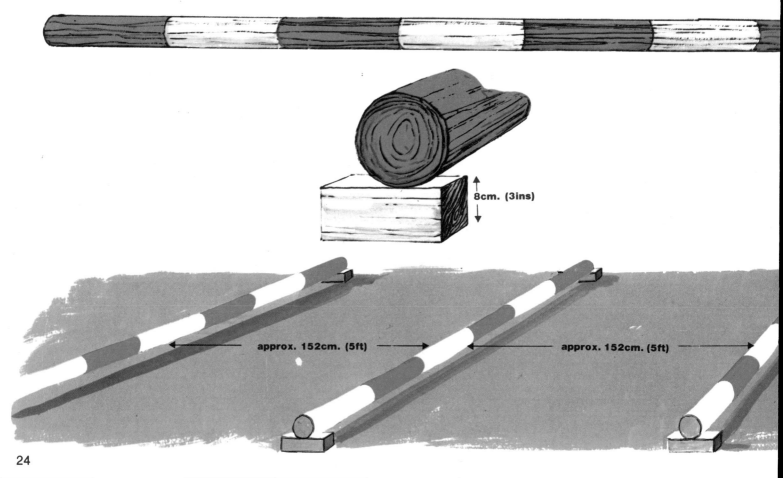

8cm. (3ins)

approx. 152cm. (5ft)   approx. 152cm. (5ft)

SCHOOLING OVER CAVALLETTI

Cavalletti are made like trestles, so that you can change the height of the cross pole when the side crosses are adjusted. On this page we give the accepted measurements for cavalletti which can be quite easily made at home.

Six cavalletti are invaluable, not only in the early stages of jumping, but throughout your riding life. International riders regularly school their horses over cavalletti.

Owning a set of cavalletti will mean you can undertake several different kinds of exercises and a variety of jumps can be built up by placing them side by side or one on top of the other.

The use of cavalletti for schooling has many advantages as they will teach you how to develop the correct riding position over jumps, combined with balance, style and strength. You will also be able to assess the actual stride being taken by your pony. To assist

you further it is best if there is an experienced person with you to guide and instruct for these and all other jumping exercises.

Cavalletti are best left unpainted. A wood preservative should be applied before putting the cavalletti to use.

To construct a cavalletto you will require some lengths of timber 76cm. (2ft 6ins) measuring 8x8cm. (3x3ins) and, either a pole or further length of 8x8cm. (3x3ins) timber measuring at least 3m. (9ft 10ins). The ends, two lengths of timber approximately 1m. (3ft) are made as shown and are bolted together. The pole is fixed into one of the cross-pieces.

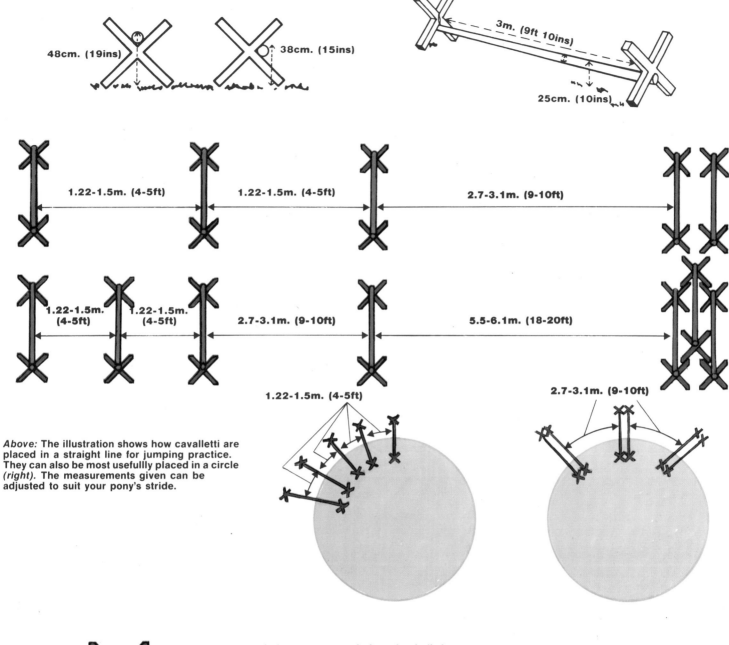

48cm. (19ins)   38cm. (15ins)

3m. (9ft 10ins)

25cm. (10ins)

1.22-1.5m. (4-5ft)   1.22-1.5m. (4-5ft)   2.7-3.1m. (9-10ft)

1.22-1.5m.
(4-5ft)   1.22-1.5m.
(4-5ft)   2.7-3.1m. (9-10ft)   5.5-6.1m. (18-20ft)

1.22-1.5m. (4-5ft)   2.7-3.1m. (9-10ft)

Above: The illustration shows how cavalletti are placed in a straight line for jumping practice. They can also be most usefullly placed in a circle *(right)*. The measurements given can be adjusted to suit your pony's stride.

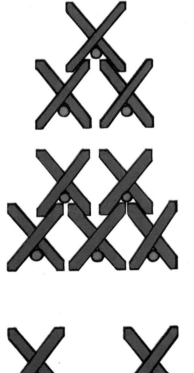

Left: some types of obstacles built from a number of cavalletti: *(top):* a pyramid; *(centre)* a spread and *(bottom)* a useful and adjustable low parallel or oxer.

PRACTICE FENCES

In practice jumping you should aim to improve the pony's style and to improve your own skill and ability. It is now that you should try to develop a judgment and understanding with each other and generate together a confidence in what you are doing.

Practice jumping must never become boring to you or your pony. It is worth remembering that in a competition you will most probably be asked to jump nine or ten fences and, if successful, jump-off over a shortened course of five or six. The time this will take will be perhaps less than three minutes in all. If you add the practice jumps you will have taken at the show before you enter the ring, you will see how unnecessary it is to spend too much time jumping over and over your own practice fences. By all means practise! But do not overdo it.

The fences illustrated here show you how easily they can be constructed. No practice fence, in the early stages, should be higher than 61 centimetres or 76 centimetres (2 feet or 2 feet 6 inches). Once you have your pony

jumping accurately, and once you feel you understand the use of the correct jumping position, it is better not to raise the height of the fence but to increase its spread. Try not to overface your pony by asking it to jump fences too high or too wide. On the other hand, it is of little value in continually practising over fences too low, or underfacing.

When constructing schooling fences, first consider the different types of obstacles. For example, fences can include those made entirely from poles, brush, bales of straw or from fallen trees.

Be sure that the ground on which you put your jumps is clear from bricks and branches and other dangerous debris. Build fences with "wings", and always try to include a ground line to assist the pony to judge his height and distance.

Do not use any fence which has jagged or rough edges; it is time well spent smoothing down poles and brush. When using poles always use thick and solid-looking ones. Horses

and ponies know only too well those they can knock down without hurting themselves!

If you decide to increase the spread, place another pole at the same height, or slightly higher, on cups or supports on the landing side. Straw bales also are a useful filling and can be made into a satisfactory jump. It is far easier for a pony to jump well-filled obstacles than those that are "open". A wall is far easier to jump than a gate.

A "double" in a practice area should be positioned where sufficient room is made for the approach, take-off and landing. A pony jumping an upright into a spread would require 6.55 metres (21 feet 6 inches) between fences, and then the same amount again to collect and move off. Of course, this distance would be adjusted where the double being taken was down or up hill. (See pages 32-33.)

Finish each practice session with a good jump no matter how small this is. Then reward your pony with a few pats on the neck and dismount, slacken the girths and allow him quietly to relax.

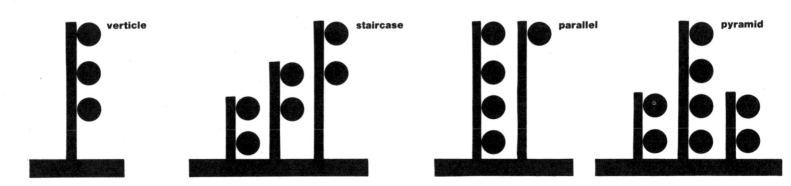

Obstacles and fences fall into four types or shapes: verticle or upright; staircase or triple-bar; parallels or near parallels; pyramids or hogs back. And, quite separately, water jumps (see page 35).

Some Practice Fences.

SHOW JUMPING

In the following pages we will be discussing the types of show jumping obstacles normally found in classes for novice riders and novice horses or ponies. We shall be discussing all important jumping techniques and the way in which to approach certain obstacles.

One of the most difficult stages in riding is making the transition from pony to horse. This may come when your pony is too small for you—or when you are too big for your pony! The choice and type of your first horse must be left to the expert, and preferably the expert who knows something of your own skill and experience as a rider.

In the remainder of this book we will talk of horses *and* ponies, since much of the rider's technique of jumping applies to either. But there is much you will have to learn, sometimes by going back to the beginning of your riding lessons and exercises, when you move out of pony classes.

It is possible that for many years you will have grown to know the exact stride of your pony; you know something of his temperament, the things he likes and those he dislikes. With a

horse these aspects have to be taught and learned again.

In the show jumping arena a pony is sometimes more adaptable. It is equally true that a horse can be more obedient. A horse will expect assistance from the rider—a pony may never accept or expect any aid and yet will jump, time after time, perfectly clear rounds!

As we have said, show jumping is fun. But the true fun will come when you have learned to be as one with your horse or pony, and when both of you set out to enjoy the challenge set by those who plan, prepare and judge, the many different types of courses built.

On the previous page we have described the four shapes of show jumping fences. In competitions these fences are made up from different coloured poles, with a variety of "filling" materials. But before you are asked to jump, you will have an opportunity to "walk the course". It is at this time that you should study the actual shape, make-up and nature of each separate obstacle.

Later in this book you will find more about "walking a course" and what you can learn when doing so.

Pony: measured on level ground from the withers to the ground, stands at 14.2hh. An extra half-inch is allowed for the shoes.

Horse: measured from the withers to the ground, stands over 14.2hh.

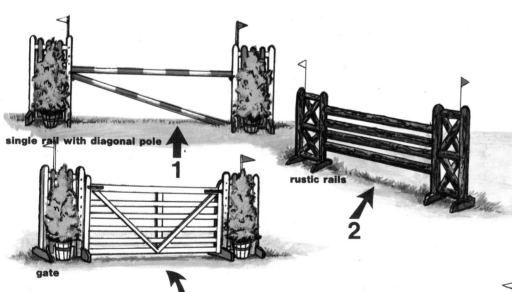

single rail with diagonal pole

1

rustic rails

2

gate

3

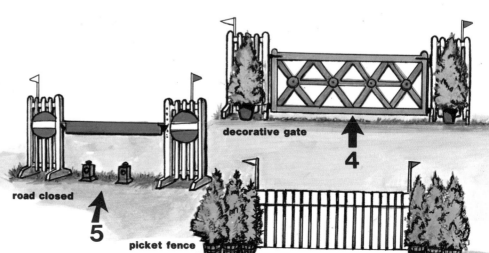

decorative gate

4

road closed

5

picket fence

Illustrated here are some of the types of fences you may find in competitive jumping rings. You should try to copy these for use in your schooling and practice periods. The arrows indicate the direction of jumping.

Where flags are placed at fences you must always jump with the red flag on your right-hand side. Flags are obligatory in marking the four corners of a water jump.

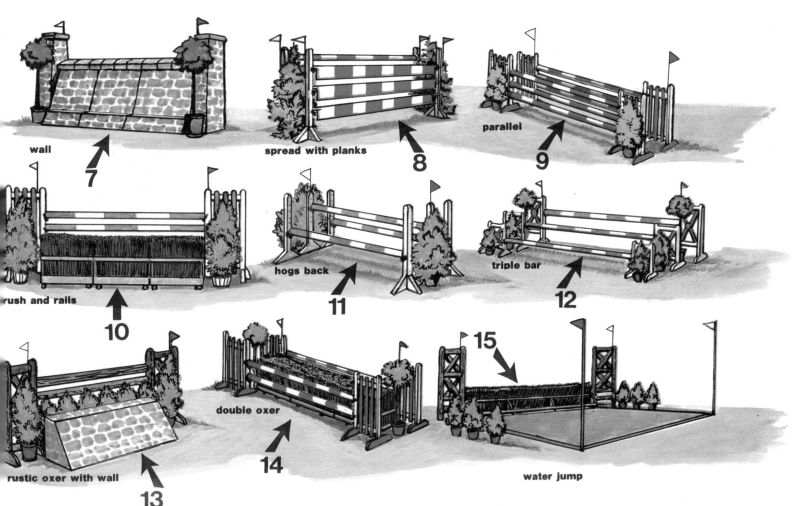

wall

7

spread with planks

8

parallel

9

rush and rails

10

hogs back

11

triple bar

12

rustic oxer with wall

13

double oxer

14

15

water jump

APPROACH AND TAKE-OFF

The position of a horse or pony as it arrives in front of an obstacle before beginning to jump is known as the point of take-off. As shown in the pictures below, there is an ideal position and point for take-off, which may vary depending on the type of obstacle.

In the jumping ring a pony will sometimes correct any mistake in his position in front of a fence without the rider necessarily having to do anything about it. Ponies are very clever at putting themselves right! A horse seldom can do this. He will expect his stride to be adjusted before the point of take-off. If not, he may refuse or run out.

To jump an upright, you should approach the fence so that your take-off point is approximately the same distance in front of the fence as the height you are about to jump. For example, to jump an upright standing at 1 metre (3 feet 3 inches) you would position your horse for take-off approximately 1 metre in front of the fence.

If you take off too near the fence, or "get underneath it", you will most likely knock the top element down with the forefeet. Taking off too early, or "standing back", may result in the hind legs "hooking" the top element when coming down for the landing.

There are no "true" measurements for a horse or pony's stride since there are many factors which may vary it. However, there are accepted "true" distances and the illustrations (opposite top) show the accepted distances for a double, with one non-jumping stride between the elements. The measurements given for both horses and ponies are those you should use when practising in your paddock or field.

A double is one type of "combination": in a treble, three separate elements or jumps make up one obstacle. In a double, the elements are positioned to permit one or two non-jumping strides between landing after the first element and taking off for the second. The distances between the elements in a treble must also be carefully measured.

In taking combinations you *must* maintain impulsion. A horse or pony, having cleared the first element has to be ridden or pushed on if he is to negotiate the second or third successfully. Far too many riders relax after the first jump. This can only lead to a refusal, knock-down or run-out.

If the first element of the double is cleared after taking off too soon, a horse or pony may require to adjust to the distance before making the second element.

On the other hand, if the horse or pony takes off too late, and then clears, he will leave himself with an odd, and perhaps more difficult half stride.

Jumping on a Slope

When a horse or pony is asked to jump a downhill track he will generally take a longer stride and therefore, depending on the angle of the slope, the distances between the elements will be increased. The reverse applies when fences are being taken uphill.

Taking a Double

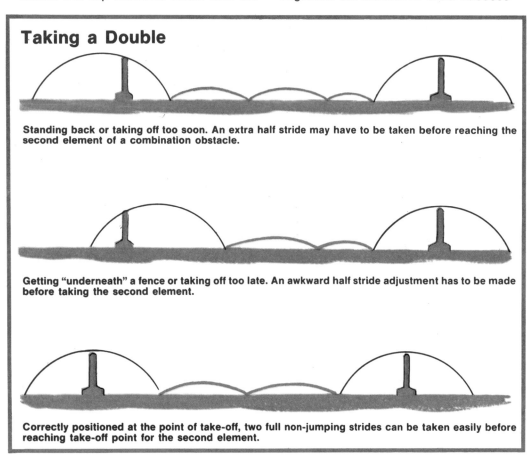

Standing back or taking off too soon. An extra half stride may have to be taken before reaching the second element of a combination obstacle.

Getting "underneath" a fence or taking off too late. An awkward half stride adjustment has to be made before taking the second element.

Correctly positioned at the point of take-off, two full non-jumping strides can be taken easily before reaching take-off point for the second element.

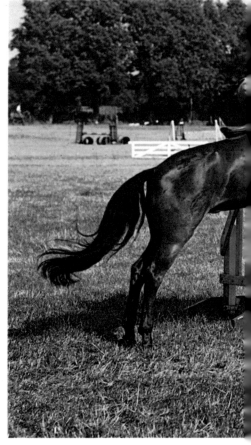

Taking Off

too soon

too late

'True' Distances

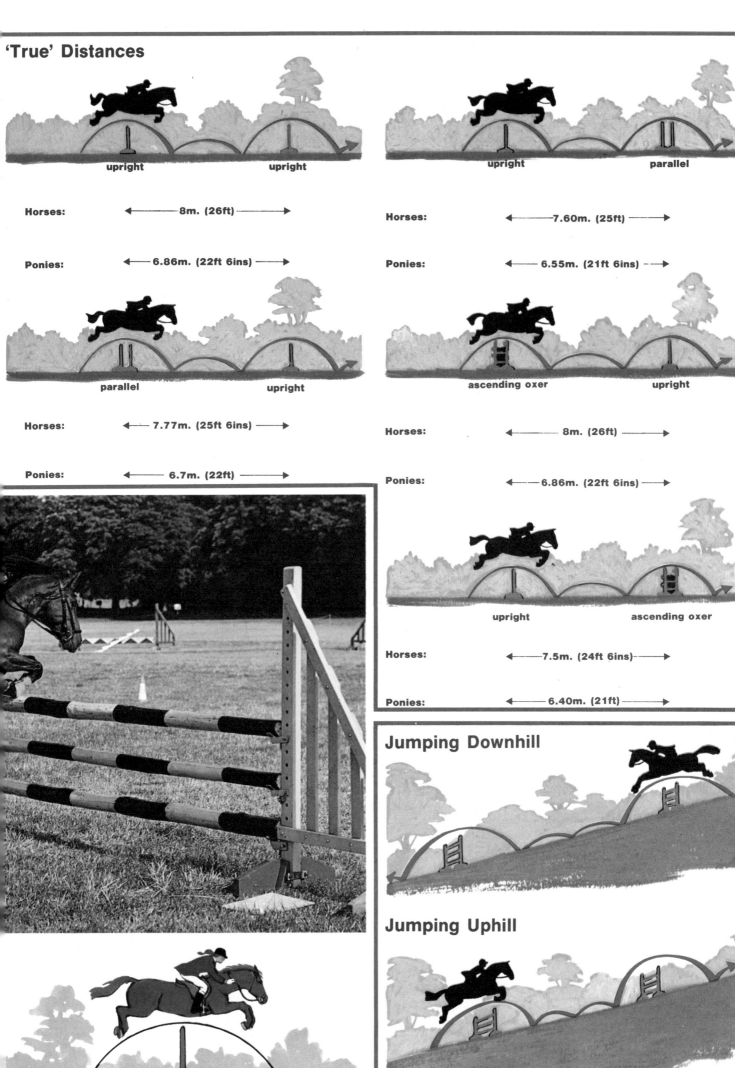

upright   **upright**

Horses:	← 8m. (26ft) →
Ponies:	← 6.86m. (22ft 6ins) →

parallel   **upright**

Horses:	← 7.77m. (25ft 6ins) →
Ponies:	← 6.7m. (22ft) →

upright   **parallel**

Horses:	← 7.60m. (25ft) →
Ponies:	← 6.55m. (21ft 6ins) →

ascending oxer   **upright**

Horses:	← 8m. (26ft) →
Ponies:	← 6.86m. (22ft 6ins) →

upright   **ascending oxer**

Horses:	← 7.5m. (24ft 6ins) →
Ponies:	← 6.40m. (21ft) →

correct

Jumping Downhill

Jumping Uphill

THE COURSE

A course should be both inviting and interesting. It should also be enjoyable. The aim is always to provide the right standard of competition, without seeking to "catch" or "trap" your mount.

Building a show jumping course either for a major international event or "the local show" is a highly skilled job. It is not simply a matter of putting different types of jumps around the ring! The choice of "track" and types of obstacle depend very much on the location, state of the going and condition of the ground.

A course builder first plans his course on paper. This is then transferred to the showground, but not until he has made a careful examination of the area of the ring and the types of competition to be jumped. Some competitions stipulate a maximum height for each round; some the maximum width for spread fences and others restrict the range of obstacles that may be included. All these factors have to be considered by the course builder.

The progression of fences a horse or pony may be asked to jump is a most important aspect of course building and calls for great skill on the part of the builder. The distance between each obstacle is very carefully measured and the "track" is planned to ensure a safe and smoothly-flowing jumping course. On the previous pages, the accepted "true" stride of a horse or pony is discussed and illustrated and this stride pattern is taken into account when placing the fences.

At indoor shows, in confined spaces, horses cannot be expected to jump without the course builder having given considerable thought to the positioning of the obstacles and to the measurements between each one.

The course illustrated here is typical of one that younger riders may encounter. Notice that it begins with an "inviting" first fence and moves steadily through different types of obstacles to finish with a measured, but more complicated combination. On the next page, you will learn how important it is to "walk the course". Riders can then study the type of course that has been built and can work out the best way to approach each fence, since the course builder will have designed it to test the rider's skill and the horse or pony's ability at each obstacle.

The Rules say that a plan of the course must be displayed at the collecting ring before the start of the competition and you should study this before you walk the course. The plan will show the distance of the track, the time allowed for jumping and, the time limit. It will also show the fences to be jumped in a jump-off, the distance and time.

Remember – you will not be given an opportunity to walk the course a second time before a jump-off. Make sure you do a thorough job before the competition starts!

WATER JUMPS

If a water jump has been included in the course, and more shows are introducing this in classes for juniors, the technique is to jump as you would a triple-bar-type fence.

You should approach the jump at an extended canter and, with good impulsion, slightly increase the speed of the canter at about four or five strides from the facing edge of the water. The take-off must be as close to the edge of the water as possible. Sit down in the saddle on your approach, using your legs and seat as strongly as you can.

At some water jumps a pole is introduced as part of the jump. If this is knocked down it will count as a fault, even though you might not have landed in the water. Remember, too, that a foot, or any part of the foot coming down on the tape or lathe on the landing side will count as a fault. However it is comforting to remember that four faults only can be given at a water jump, even though you might knock down the cross pole and come down in the water!

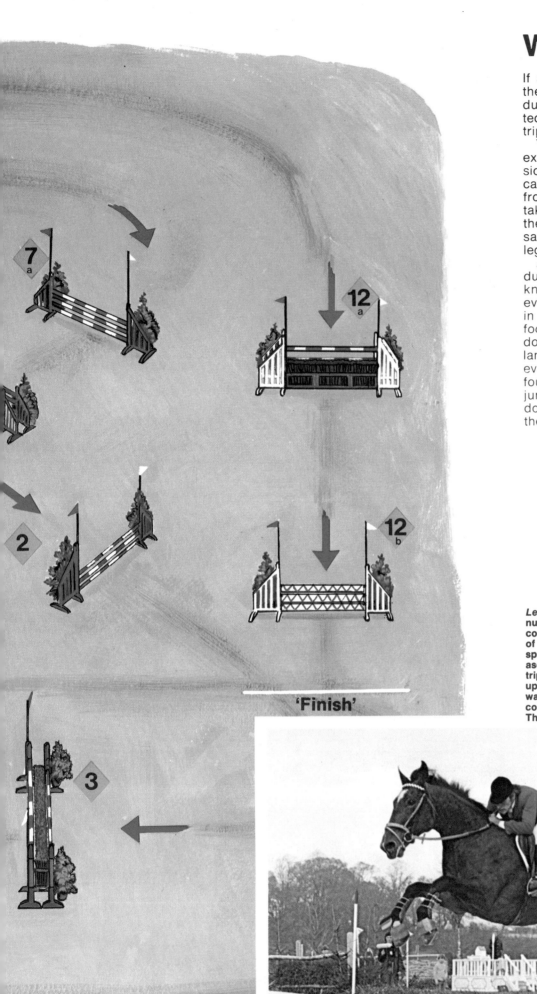

'Finish'

Left: A typical show jumping course. The fence numbers are given as a guidance only: on the course, they would appear on the right hand side of the fences. 1. an inviting fence, usually a spread; 2. an upright with a ground line; 3. an ascending oxer; 4. an upright of planks; 5. a triple bar; 6. gate; 7. a double, comprising an upright to a parallel; 8. crossed poles; 9. wall; 10. water jump; 11. spread oxer; 12. a double, comprising an oxer to an upright of planks. Then, through to the Finish!

THE HORSE SHOW

Many weeks before a horse show takes place, the organisers will have planned the entire day and produced a schedule of events and classes. They will have dealt with the ground, rings, jumps, catering and the hundred and one things that go to make a successful show.

You become involved with the show the moment you have a schedule and decide which classes you will enter. There is a wide choice to choose from now that jumping competitions take place throughout the year, and all sizes and types of ponies are catered for.

Some shows will have competitions for ponies not exceeding 12.2hh, and for those between 12.2hh and 13.2hh,

or 13.2hh and 14.2hh. The schedule might indicate that some riders and ponies are not allowed to enter, for example, those who may have already won a first place in a previous jumping competition, or who may have won prize money beyond a certain figure. The local rules and conditions of entry are always included in the schedule, and these, together with the information about each separate class, must be studied.

Then the day arrives!

Get to the showground early. Give yourself plenty of time to collect your jumping number and look at the way the show has been laid out. Check where the rings are sited and where

the practice area is. If you have not travelled by horse-box or trailer, find a suitable spot where there will be shade and where you can tie up your horse or pony when not competing. Remember your horse or pony will require some hay or feed during the day and most certainly, water. Be sure all this is available.

Soon after you have given your number to the collecting ring steward and found your place in the jumping order, you will be invited to "walk the course". This, for show jumpers, is a most important part of the day, for you now have an opportunity to see what type of course has been built, what types of fences have been included, what changes of rein are necessary and what measurements have been included in doubles and elsewhere. Walk the track, which is not the same as walking from fence to fence! The track is the line the course builder and judges believe is the correct way the course should be jumped—it is never the shortest line, it is the one for which distance and time has been assessed.

The distances between obstacles, measured by your own strides and then worked out against the stride of your horse or pony, should be carefully noted.

When you are called to enter the ring do so quietly and wait for the bell or hooter before starting your round. Before you enter the ring, it is advisable to have watched other competitors jumping the course. In this way you will see where they might be coming up against any problems or difficulties you did not spot when you walked the course.

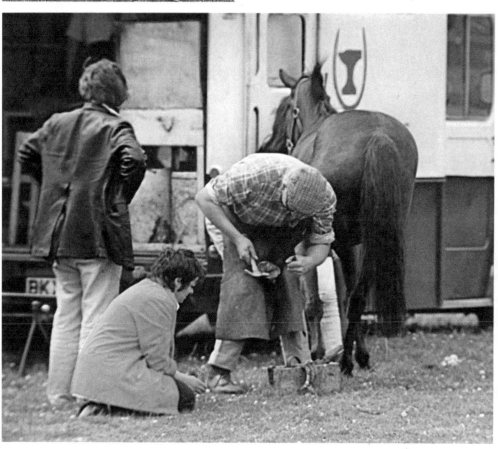

Above: **A first look at the showground! This delightful pony is taking an early opportunity to see what all the fuss is about.**
(above right): **Time for a quiet feed between classes.** *(right):* **at most shows a farrier is available to replace lost shoes and to carry out minor repairs.**

Left: In the ring and jumping well. A clear round? Some faults, perhaps? Whatever the result, both horse and rider will have tried their best.
(bottom): A rider loosens the girths after jumping, before taking her mount back to the horse-box. *(below):* A happy moment for this successful competitor receiving a rosette – a reward for much hard work and training.

If you jump a clear round, you will have to wait for a jump-off, provided you are not the only clear round! A jump-off will take place where more than one rider has either a clear round or the same number of faults and is equal in first place.

A jump-off is usually ridden against time and takes place over a shortened course. You should know the fences to be included, for you are not allowed to "walk" a jump-off course. An order of jumping will be drawn by the judges, and this order must be kept. You will be eliminated if you are not ready to jump when called.

In the shortened course, and with time being so important, you may decide where you can cut corners. It is not always possible to save time by taking the shortest route. A horse or pony could be put off balance by being brought into a fence too short or not straight which could result in a refusal —and you couldn't blame him for that! The track you take in a jump-off should be your choice!

The most important thing about entering a jumping competition is taking part, whether or not you win a rosette. Taking part, that is, in one of the most exacting and exciting sports of all.

EVENTING AND COMBINED TRAINING

To take part in eventing your pony must be able to undertake a dressage test, to jump a cross-country course and finally to jump a normal show-jumping course. Marks are awarded in each phase and the winner is the rider with the best score overall.

Eventing usually takes place over one day, though experienced riders compete in three-day events such as Badminton or Burghley. Also spread across three days are the European and World Championships and, of course, the Olympic Games.

At a one-day event you would begin in the morning with a dressage test, which is set according to the standard

Top (right): HRH Princess Anne riding Goodwill in the dressage phase at the Crookham Horse Trials. **(above):** Janet Hodgson on Larkspur going through the water at Burghley. **(right):** Richard Meade, reigning Olympic Champion, jumping at Badminton.

of the entire competition, Dressage is a systematic method of training for both pony and rider. The movements involved are those which are carried out in ordinary riding and schooling, such as walk, trot, canter, turns, halt and rein-back, and in which balance plays an important part. A dressage competition is a test of horsemanship carried out in a specially prepared and marked out arena.

Each country has a series of dressage tests which range from elementary to advance *haute ecole,* or high school. If you take a dressage test, you should select the most appropriate test according to the standard you have reached. You should write to the British Horse Society if you would like full details of the test sheets available.

Next will follow the cross-country phase where you will be expected to jump a course of ditches, gates, fallen trees, water and other natural obstacles. In the afternoon, to show your horse or pony is still supple and obedient, you will jump one round over a fairly straight-forward show-jumping course.

Top: **A young rider during her dressage phase.** *(left):* **Negotiating successfully a difficult drop fence at Crookham.** *(above):* **An excellent jump at the parallel.**

At a three-day event, the separate phases of dressage, cross-country and show jumping take place on con-secutive days.

Combined training events do not

HUNTER TRIALS

Hunter trials, usually staged during the autumn and spring are cross-country jumping events, in which all the obstacles are of the type which may be found when out hunting. All the fences are solidly-constructed and are natural looking—you would seldom find a coloured pole! At most hunter trials the fences are fixed, in other words, there are no poles to knock down or dislodge from cups.

The organisers of hunter trials are invariably from the local Hunt and classes are arranged for many different standards of riding: from the beginner to the more advanced, and from the younger riders to those who have considerable experience. Most hunter trials take place on farming land and consequently have a mixture of wooded country and good open "going". There may well be water to jump, and it is almost certain that there will be some jumps to take going down a slope and some going uphill.

Having decided on the event and, having spent some of the previous day walking the course, it is well to know something of the judging procedure.

The distance of a "trial" is measured and this with the expected riding speed is displayed on a notice near to the start or by the judges' car or caravan. Suppose for example that a course is 1200 metres long (1300 yards). If the speed required is 300 metres (325 yards) per minute you would then be able to work out that the best time to finish would be exactly four minutes after starting, with no penalties, of course! The notice will also indicate the penalties which might well be added or deducted from the time total. For example, a refusal at any fence may incur 10 penalties; a fall, 20 penalties. A run out, not corrected, will mean elimination. Study very closely the local rules and conditions, since these will give you some relevant information about the competition and the way the competition will be judged.

Judges are posted at each fence. They will note whether or not you refuse or run out—and trust that you will not fall! Some of the fence judges may look for "hunting style", a mix of the pace and method of approach and take-off you make at each particular fence.

The winner of this type of riding competition which is becoming increasingly popular throughout the world, is the one who has scored nearest to the "bogey" total set. Even if you cannot take part in hunter trials, do try and go along as a spectator—its great fun and you will have a most enjoyable and invigorating day!

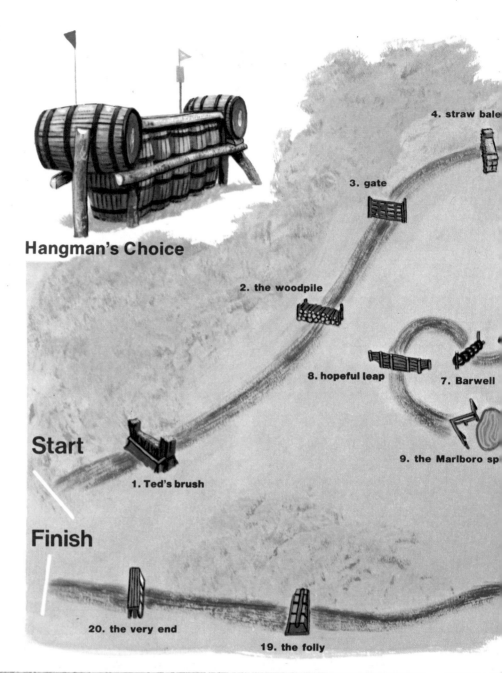

Hangman's Choice

4. straw bale

3. gate

2. the woodpile

8. hopeful leap

7. Barwell

Start

9. the Marlboro spi

1. Ted's brush

Finish

20. the very end

19. the folly

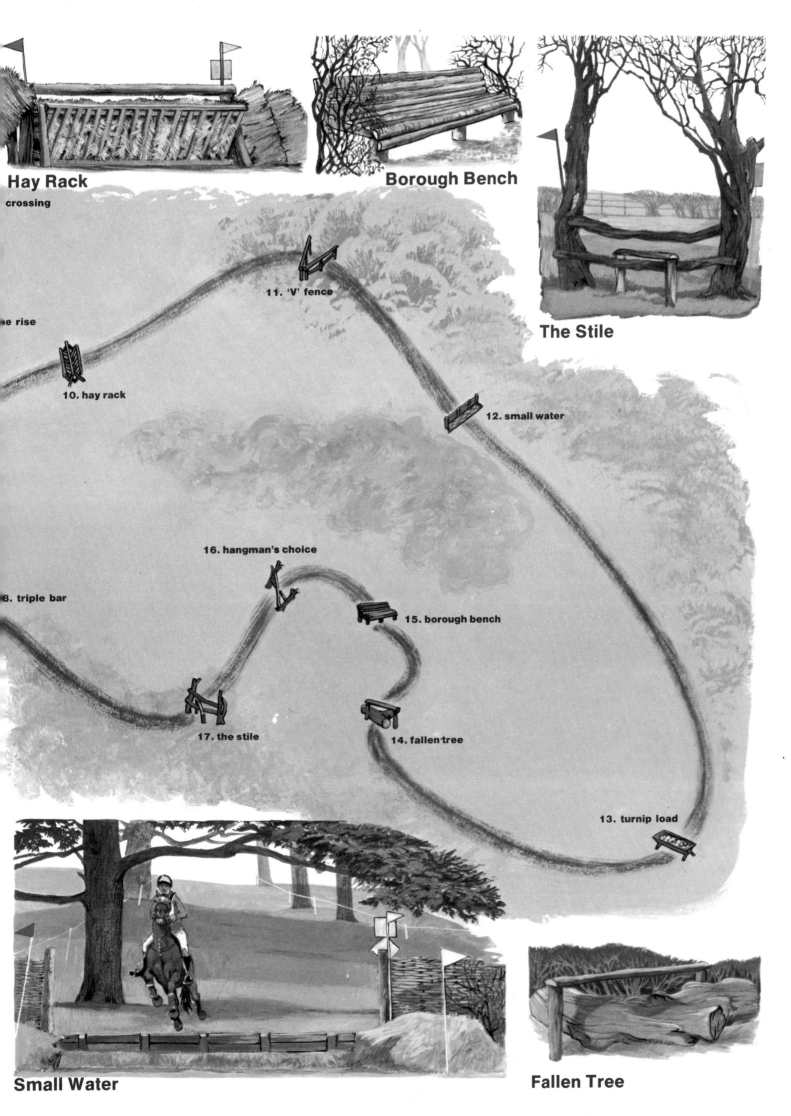

Hay Rack

crossing

Borough Bench

The Stile

11. 'V' fence

...e rise

10. hay rack

12. small water

16. hangman's choice

8. triple bar

15. borough bench

17. the stile

14. fallen tree

13. turnip load

Small Water

Fallen Tree

A FEW RULES TO REMEMBER

To many younger riders the rules of show jumping appear complicated and involved. But this is not really so, and a study of the Rules and Regulations published by the British Show Jumping Association is a *must,* as most competitions held at horse shows in the United Kingdom are judged by these rules. The Fédération Equestre Internationale (FEI) also produce a Rule Book which covers the international competitions, many of which are televised during the year.

It is important that the Rules of all jumping and riding disciplines are understood. It is also essential that the Rules and Conditions laid down by each Show and printed in the schedules are read and followed.

We illustrate on these pages some of the rules of showjumping which are not always clear to younger riders. Most penalties are for refusals or knockdowns, but the Rules of the British Show Jumping Association and the Fédération Equestre Internationale also list more than twenty ways a competitor may be eliminated! Read the rule books carefully, and then enjoy your jumping!

Refusal

If a pony stops in front of an obstacle and, without knocking it down and without reining back immediately jumps from a standing position, there is no penalty. But should the pony be reined back, even a single pace, a refusal is considered to have been made.

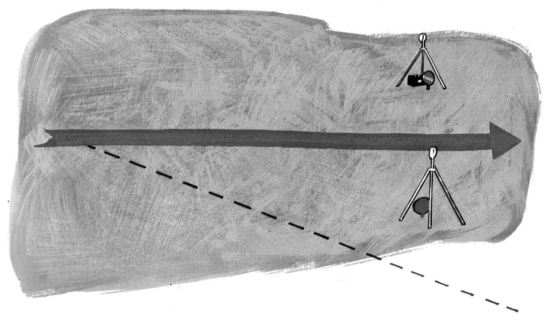

Failing to go through 'Start' or 'Finish'

A competitor will be eliminated if he fails to go through the start line within 45 seconds of being given the order to start. He will also be eliminated should he fail to go through the finish mounted, in the right direction.

At a Water Jump

It is a fault when a pony lands in the water or on the lathe or tape, with any part of a foot.

Right

Wrong

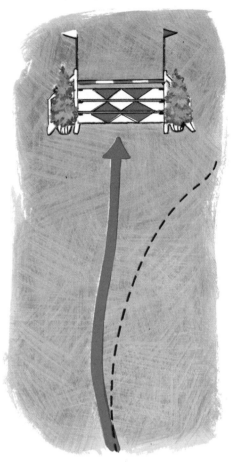

Run Out

One of the many disobediences which can occur in show jumping. A pony avoids the obstacle by running out.

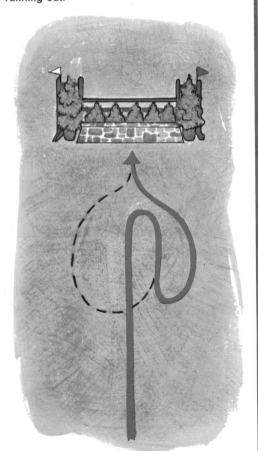

Turning a Circle

It will count as a disobedience if a pony makes a circle, before jumping the next obstacle, that is when a pony crosses his track. A pony may circle once or more than once without penalty if this is done after a run-out or a disobedience in order to re-take the correct track.

Jumping the Wrong Course

Should a competitor jump, or attempt to jump, an obstacle in the wrong order or miss out an obstacle and jump, or attempt to jump the next, he will be eliminated.

Fall of Pony or Rider

A pony is considered to have fallen when the shoulder and quarters on the same side touch the ground. A rider is considered to have fallen when there is a separation between him and his pony, which will mean he will have to re-mount. The penalty for a fall of either pony or rider or both is eight faults.

TOP RIDERS IN ACTION

Here are some pictures of well-known international riders and their horses during various competitions. You will notice the different styles adopted when jumping but all have the same determined concentration. *Right:* A brilliant jump by Wayfarer, ridden by Richard Meade. *(below):* Anne Moore on the consistent Psalm.

Above: **The reigning World Champion, Harwig Steenken (Germany) on Simona.** *(right):* **David Broome, World Champion from 1970-1974, on Sportsman at Hickstead.**

Above (left): Holder of the Men's European Championship, Paddy McMahon, jumps clear with Pennwood Forge Mill. (right): From Holland, the skilful Johan Heinz with Kim at Hickstead in 1974.

45